ideals® CHRISTMAS

More Than 50 Years of Celebrating Life's Most Treasured Moments

Vol. 54, No. 6

"We are better throughout the year for having, in spirit, become a child again at Christmastime."

—Laura Ingalls Wilder

IDEALS—Vol. 54, No. 6 November MCMXCVII IDEALS (ISSN 0019-137X) is published six times a year: January, March, May, July, September, and November by IDEALS PUBLICATIONS INCORPORATED, 535 Metroplex Drive, Suite 250, Nashville, TN 37211.
Periodical postage paid at Nashville, Tennessee, and additional mailing offices.

SINGLE ISSUE—U.S. $5.95 USD; Higher in Canada
ONE-YEAR SUBSCRIPTION—U.S. $19.95 USD; Canada $36.00 CDN (incl. GST and shipping); Foreign $25.95 USD
TWO-YEAR SUBSCRIPTION—U.S. $35.95 USD; Canada $66.50 CDN (incl. GST and shipping); Foreign $47.95 USD

Printed and bound in USA by Quebecor Printing. Printed on Weyerhaeuser Husky.

The paper used in this publication meets the minimum requirements of American National Standard for Information Sciences—Permanence of Paper for Printed Library Materials, ANSI Z39.48-1984.

Subscribers may call customer service at 1-800-558-4343 to make address changes.
Unsolicited manuscripts will not be returned without a self-addressed, stamped envelope.

ISBN 0-8249-1146-6 GST 131903775

Cover Photo
SNOW ON CHRISTMAS EVE
Cape Cod, Massachusetts
William Johnson/Johnson's Photography

Inside Covers
HEAVENLY SONG AND *HARP SONG*
Original oil paintings by Donald Zolan
© 1996 Zolan Fine Arts, Ltd.
Hershey, Pennsylvania

Christmas Trees

Robert Frost

The city had withdrawn into itself
And left at last the country to the country;
When between whirls of snow not come to lie
And whirls of foliage not yet laid, there drove
A stranger to our yard, who looked the city,
Yet did in country fashion in that there
He sat and waited till he drew us out,
A-buttoning coats, to ask him who he was.
He proved to be the city come again
To look for something it had left behind
And could not do without and keep its Christmas.
He asked if I would sell my Christmas trees;
My woods—the young fir balsams like a place
Where houses all are churches and have spires.
I hadn't thought of them as Christmas trees.
I doubt if I was tempted for a moment
To sell them off their feet to go in cars
And leave the slope behind the house all bare,
Where the sun shines now no warmer than the moon.
I'd hate to have them know it if I was.
Yet more I'd hate to hold my trees, except
As others hold theirs or refuse for them,
Beyond the time of profitable growth—
The trial by market everything must come to.
I dallied so much with the thought of selling.
Then whether from mistaken courtesy
And fear of seeming short of speech, or whether
From hope of hearing good of what was mine,
I said, "There aren't enough to be worth my while."

"I could soon tell how many they would cut,
You let me look them over."

"You could look.
But don't expect I'm going to let you have them."
Pasture they spring in, some in clumps too close
That lop each other of boughs, but not a few
Quite solitary and having equal boughs
All round and round. The latter he nodded "Yes" to,
Or paused to say beneath some lovelier one,
With a buyer's moderation, "That would do."
I thought so too, but wasn't there to say so.
We climbed the pasture on the south, crossed over,
And came down on the north.

He said, "A thousand."

"A thousand Christmas trees!—at what apiece?"

He felt some need of softening that to me:
"A thousand trees would come to thirty dollars."

Then I was certain I had never meant
To let him have them. Never show surprise!
But thirty dollars seemed so small beside
The extent of pasture I should strip, three cents
(For that was all they figured out apiece)—
Three cents so small beside the dollar friends
I should be writing to within the hour
Would pay in cities for good trees like those,
Regular vestry-trees whole Sunday Schools
Could hang enough on to pick off enough.

A thousand Christmas trees I didn't know I had!
Worth three cents more to give away than sell,
As may be shown by a simple calculation.
Too bad I couldn't lay one in a letter.
I can't help wishing I could send you one
In wishing you herewith a Merry Christmas.

TRAIN TRESTLE
Cloudcroft, New Mexico
Josiah Davidson Scenic Photography

Deepening Snow

Anna Belle Jeffries

Snowflakes gently fall around me
As I walk in shimm'ring white;
Silence permeates the landscape
On this cold and starry night.

Muffled in the land of winter
Are my footsteps as I go
Down the road that takes me homeward
Through the ever-deep'ning snow.

As snow fills each nook and cranny,
Not a bird nor creature stirs
From its little sheltered dwelling
In or under mighty firs.

In this season of white beauty,
When the worldly din is stilled
By the snowflakes flung from heaven,
With blessed peace the land is filled.

Winter hangs her icy festoons
Everywhere, for all to see;
Moonlight sparkles through the prisms
Trimming every bush and tree.

Frozen lace adorns the lampposts
As they set the path aglow
With their golden orbs of lamplight
Flickering in falling snow.

In the distance like a beacon,
Lights of home at last I see;
Eagerly I hurry onward
To the warmth awaiting me.

DECEMBER EVENING
Near Lancaster, Pennsylvania
Larry LeFever/Grant Heilman Photography

Etudes in Winter White

Lon Myruski

Bewitching wintry wind songs rake
The argent woodland realm
With harmonies through hoary boughs
Of rimy oak and elm.
Fine snow swirls swish in rising like
A silky dancing dress
To fall softly into silence—
A waning humoresque.

Glazed icicles on evergreens
Collide, kissed by a breeze—
Enchanting crystal bells that chime
Breathtaking melodies.
And trickling rills and rivulets
Compose orchestral scores;
Their waters sighing in a froth
Of winter-white encores.

Overleaf Photograph
GLADE CREEK GRISTMILL
Babcock State Park, West Virginia
Josiah Davidson Photography

WAHKEENA FALLS
Columbia River Gorge National Scenic Area, Oregon
Steve Terrill Photography

Readers' Reflections

Editor's Note: Readers are invited to submit unpublished, original poetry for possible publication in future issues of Ideals. *Please send typed copies only; manuscripts will not be returned. Writers receive $10 for each published submission. Send material to* Readers' Reflections, Ideals Publications Inc., P. O. Box 305300, Nashville, Tennessee 37230-5300.

ODYSSEY

If I could be a child again,
 I'd take the road to Bethlehem.
I'd find the stable cold and bare
 And kneel before the Christ Child there.
I'd give to Him a cheerful song
 That He could sing when things went wrong.
I'd give to Him my treasure chest
 That's filled with things I love the best—
Some shells I found along the shore,
 Some pretty stones, and one thing more:
The gift of laughter He could share
 With all sad people everywhere.

Please let me be a child again;
 I'll walk the road to Bethlehem.
And should I chance someone to meet
 Along that cold and lonely street,
Should they be weary, ill, or old,
 I'll give to them my gift of gold.
Precious metal? No, not mine;
 The gift of caring, true and fine.
Then I shall hear in cadence fair
 The song I thought I'd lost somewhere.

Marcia Bierie
Massillon, Ohio

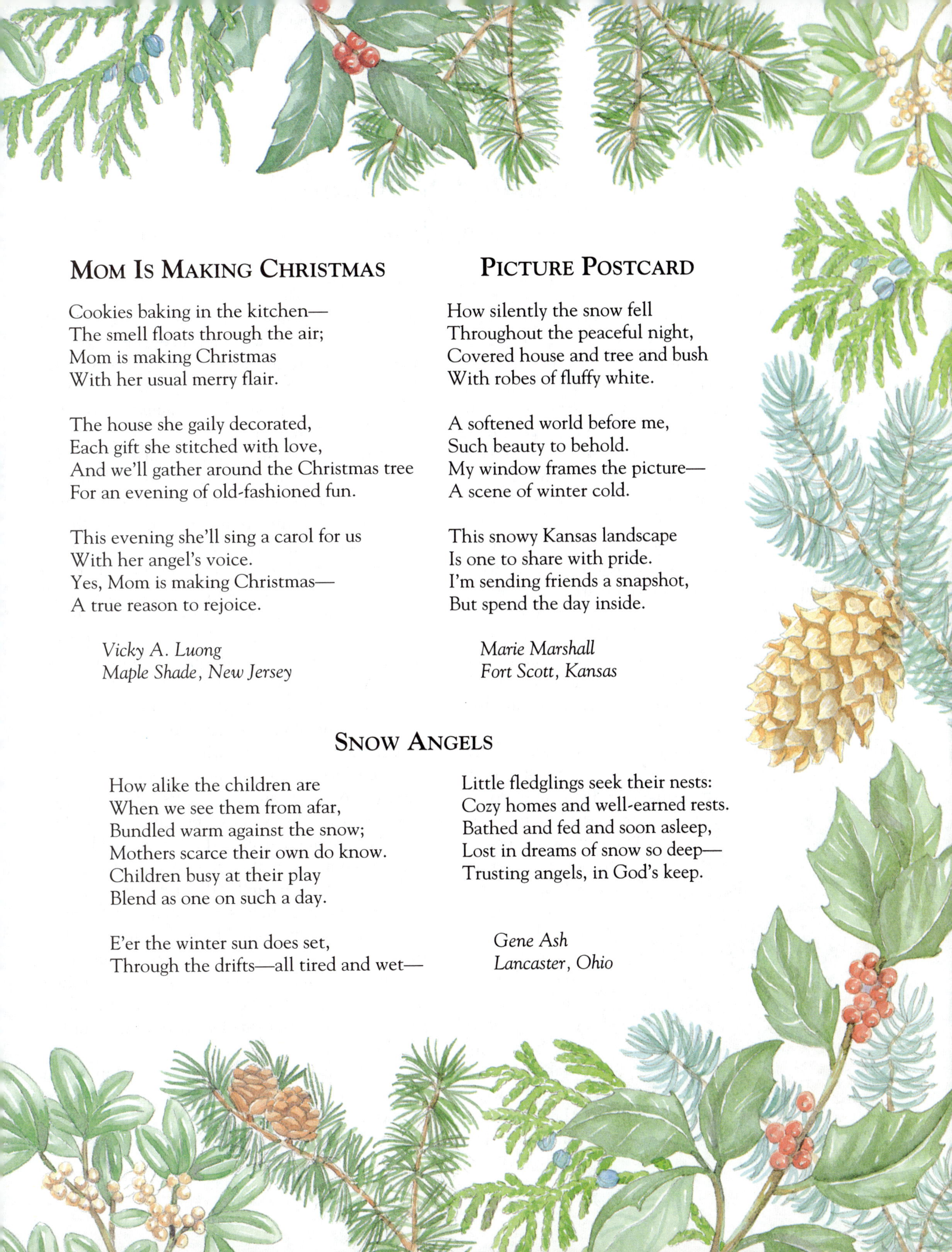

Mom Is Making Christmas

Cookies baking in the kitchen—
The smell floats through the air;
Mom is making Christmas
With her usual merry flair.

The house she gaily decorated,
Each gift she stitched with love,
And we'll gather around the Christmas tree
For an evening of old-fashioned fun.

This evening she'll sing a carol for us
With her angel's voice.
Yes, Mom is making Christmas—
A true reason to rejoice.

Vicky A. Luong
Maple Shade, New Jersey

Picture Postcard

How silently the snow fell
Throughout the peaceful night,
Covered house and tree and bush
With robes of fluffy white.

A softened world before me,
Such beauty to behold.
My window frames the picture—
A scene of winter cold.

This snowy Kansas landscape
Is one to share with pride.
I'm sending friends a snapshot,
But spend the day inside.

Marie Marshall
Fort Scott, Kansas

Snow Angels

How alike the children are
When we see them from afar,
Bundled warm against the snow;
Mothers scarce their own do know.
Children busy at their play
Blend as one on such a day.

E'er the winter sun does set,
Through the drifts—all tired and wet—
Little fledglings seek their nests:
Cozy homes and well-earned rests.
Bathed and fed and soon asleep,
Lost in dreams of snow so deep—
Trusting angels, in God's keep.

Gene Ash
Lancaster, Ohio

From My Garden Journal

by Deana Deck

Dwarf Conifers

I have a number of close friends who have recently sold their homes and moved into smaller condominiums or town houses. Some have vacation homes elsewhere, but the majority will be living year-round in their new dwellings. Invariably one of the reasons they always give for making the decision to move is the desire to give up the chores of tending a large lawn in favor of a smaller garden. I've come to expect the phone call that comes right after my friends have settled in, when they always ask, "What should I plant?" The evergreen trees and shrubs that adorned those huge suburban lawns and helped anchor the homes to the landscape just won't fit in a small space. Yet there's something amiss about a garden with no year-round greenery. The answer many are discovering is dwarf conifers.

Dwarf conifers are miniature versions of the familiar evergreens used for foundation plantings, hedges, and focal points in larger landscape plans. There are a number of species to choose from, all varying in their hardiness. Be sure to select the one that suits your climate zone. Among those readily available, beginning with the hardiest variety, are dwarf Pfitzer Juniper (*Juniperus x media*, Pfitzer); dwarf Alberta or white spruce (*Picea glauca*, Conica); dwarf Japanese yew (*T. cuspidata*, Nana); dwarf Siberian pine, also known as Japanese stone pine (*Pinus pumila*); and the dwarf English yew (*Taxus baccata*, Nana).

Although most of these plants are cold-weather hardy, none of them fare well in the warmest regions of the country. They are, however, perfectly suited to use in containers, which gives them a mighty advantage over ordinary evergreens. For one thing, they seldom reach heights of more than four or five feet, and some do not grow more than three feet tall. All are slow-growing specimens that can be kept containerized for years with proper pruning and care. And they are highly portable.

This last factor is advantageous because it means the plants can be shifted about from season to season. In spring when bulbs are putting on their show, dwarf conifers can be moved to a sunny spot to await their center-stage appearance after the bulb foliage begins to fade. During the summer, the potted conifers are ideal for anchoring an annual bed, especially if the garden is enclosed in high walls and requires a vertical reference to help screen blank wall space. Once clematis and other flowering vines go dormant in winter, their place can be taken by an artfully arranged grouping of containerized dwarf conifers. Or you can move the plant indoors for use as a small Christmas tree during the holidays.

Even though dwarf evergreens don't lose their leaves, they do all go dormant in winter. Sap drains from the branches into the root system to help the plant survive cold weather. For this reason, it's important to plan on keeping a potted dwarf conifer indoors for no more than a week. Any longer and you will need to put it into a holding place after the holidays. A garage or storage shed will suffice, and the plant will need to rest there for several days, protected from extreme cold and drying winds, while it reacclimates itself to winter weather. Instead of bothering with reacclimating my plants, I prefer to have a pair of matching dwarf conifers in the garden that can take turns coming indoors for Christmas. Each can spend a week or so in the house and then change places with its twin.

Containerized evergreens are very susceptible to drying out in windy weather, but this problem can be prevented with an annual spraying of a desiccant, available at most hardware stores and garden centers under a variety of brand names. Application of a desiccant is essential when the plant is moved indoors for use as a holiday decoration. Evergreens tend to lose moisture through their leaves year-round, although the process slows considerably from fall until spring. However, once you move the plant into a warm house, the process will accelerate.

If your potted dwarf conifers will be spending the winter outdoors, they will still require moisture. When extremely hard freezes are predicted, soak the soil in the container. It will freeze and the roots will be held at a tolerable 32° F until the cold spell passes.

In hot summer weather, containerized evergreens will require watering on an almost daily basis. Because oxygen is essential for the health of plant roots, the soil in your containers should be loose and well-draining and needs to be kept evenly moist without drowning the root system. There is no handy rule of thumb for how much water potted conifers require, for moisture needs depend on temperature, wind, and location. In general, the plants can tell you what they need. The youngest and most tender leaves will begin to wilt if you provide too little water. If you water too heavily, the tops of the plants will begin to wilt and die because the feeder roots, those nearest the surface, are drowning and are unable to transport water upward to the foliage.

Dwarf conifers can be shaped by careful pruning and training. One of the most popular forms appearing on the market today is the spiral juniper, which is often used to frame front doors. Others can be trained inside topiary frames to a number of geometric shapes.

But many dwarf-conifer enthusiasts prefer the plant's traditional shape, which makes it a perfect miniature Christmas tree. Unlike a six-foot-tall spruce, a dwarf conifer used for a Christmas tree looks best with a minimum of decorations, perhaps a simple star or angel on top and a single spiral of red or gold ribbon twined from top to bottom. Decorated dwarf conifers make lovely holiday additions to a guest bedroom or child's room as well and will make a nice Christmas Eve surprise. If you choose not to bring your plants indoors, consider lining them up outside a sliding glass door, decorated with simple white lights or emphasized with artfully placed spotlights.

Whether you hope to personalize a large yard, create a focal point for a small winter garden, or add a delightful touch to your holiday decor, dwarf conifers are the perfect solution. Few plants offer such year-round enjoyment and versatility. And besides, potted dwarf conifers are the one Christmas decoration you won't have to put back in the attic.

Deana Deck tends to her flowers, plants, and vegetables at her home in Nashville, Tennessee, where her popular garden column is a regular feature in The Tennessean.

Country Christmas

Ruth K. Stroh

Christmas is snow on the rail fence and pine;
Christmas is icicles' sparkle and shine,
Mistletoe, crowfoot, and red-berried holly,
Carols and friendship and everything jolly.
Christmas is candles and fragile glass balls,
Firelight flickers on knotty pine walls.
Christmas is letting the dogs in the house
And sharing our feast of turkey and grouse.
Christmas is jingle bells, angels, and joy,
A laugh with a toy from a girl or a boy.
Christmas is bright tinsel strung on a tree,
Popcorn and cookies and much jamboree.
Christmas is magic wherever it's found,
Giving and sharing when goodies abound.
Christmas is memories mellow and pleasant,
Finding quaint cards with a quail or a pheasant.
Christmas is starlight, dream light, and love—
A small bit of heaven come down from above.

Christmas is hope in the hearts of all men
That peace will return to the earth once again!

WINTER AFTERNOON
Craftsbury Commons, Vermont
Ron Thomas/FPG International

G O I
R Q 8
1 N K

Christmas Giving

Iris W. Bray

Christmas is for giving
And for showing that we care,
For honoring the Christ Child
With the loving gifts we share.

The wise men gave of riches;
The shepherds, faith and love.
Each gift, in its own measure,
Was smiled on from above.

Let every gift be treasured;
Not always size or price
Determines the extent of love
And willing sacrifice.

Handsome gifts with festive trim
Bring smiles of sweet content,
But modest gifts of humble means
Are ofttimes heaven sent.

Whether it be large or small,
Each gift will share in part
The message of true Christmas joy
If given from the heart!

Gifts

Weldon Taylor Hammond

If God will give me childlike faith,
The love that spans the second mile,
His grace to overcome my faults
And bear my heartaches with a smile,
If He will grant me fortitude
To form a soul of sterling worth—
I'll hail these as the greatest gifts
A mortal can receive on earth!

ANTIQUE TOYS
A. Teufen
H. Armstrong Roberts

Bits & Pieces

We do not obtain the most precious gifts
by going in search of them but by waiting for them.

Simone Weil

Love is higher than the other
gifts in value. . . . It is not dependent
on ability, popularity, or shrewdness.
The greatest path is open to the least of travelers.

Erwin W. Lutzer

Love is not getting, but giving.

Henry van Dyke

Love ever gives,
Forgives, outlives,
And ever stands
With open hands.
And while it lives,
It gives.
For this is love's prerogative—
Oh, give, and give, and give.

John Oxenham

As we give, we live.

Sidney Greenberg

You can give without loving,
but you cannot love without giving.

Amy Carmichael

And when they had opened their treasures,
they presented unto him gifts; gold,
and frankincense, and myrrh.

Matthew 2:11

An easy thing, O Power divine,
To thank Thee for these gifts of Thine,
For summer's sunshine, winter's snow,
For hearts that kindle, thoughts that glow;
But when shall I attain to this—
To thank Thee for the things I miss?

Thomas Wentworth Storrow Higginson

Kindness in giving creates love.

Lao-tse

Each day comes bearing its gifts,
Untie the ribbons.

Ann Ruth Schabacker

Remember When

from Christmas in Maine

Robert P. Tristram Coffin

If you want to have a Christmas like the one we had on Paradise Farm when I was a boy, you will have to hunt up a salt-water farm on the Maine coast, with bays on both sides of it, and a road that goes around all sorts of bays, up over Misery Hill and down, and through the fir trees so close together that they brush you and your horse on both cheeks. That is the only kind of place a Christmas like that grows. . . .

There will be a lot of aunts in the house. . . . Aunts of every complexion and cut. Christmas is the one time that even the most dubious of aunts takes on value. One of them can make up wreaths, another can make rock candy that puts a tremble on the heart, and still another can steer your twelve-seater bob-sled—and turn it over, bottom up, with you all in just the right place for a fine spill.

There will be uncles, too, to hold one end of the molasses taffy you will pull sooner or later, yanking it out till it flashes and turns into cornsilk that almost floats in the air, tossing your end of it back and probably lassoing your uncle around his neck as you do it, and pulling out a new rope of solid honey. . . .

There will be cousins by the cart load. He-ones and she-ones. The size you can sit on, and the size that can sit on you. Enough for two

armies, on Little Round Top and on Big, up in the haymow. You will play Gettysburg there till your heads are full of hay chaff that will keep six aunts busy cleaning it out. And then you will come in to the house and down a whole crock of molasses cookies—the kind that go up in peaks in the middle—which somebody was foolish enough to leave the cover off. . . .

The whole nation of you in the house will go from one thing to another. The secret of the best Christmases is everybody doing the same things all at the same time. You will all fall to and string cranberries and popcorn for the tree, and the bright lines each of you has a hold on will radiate from the tree like ribbons on a maypole. Everybody will have needles and thread in the mouth, you will all get in each other's way, but that is the art of doing Christmas right. . . .

Then you had best find a fair substitute for my father. Give him the best chair in the house—and the way to find *that* is to push the cat out of it—and let him tear! He will begin by telling you about such people as the brilliant young ladies of Philadelphia who had a piano too big to fit their house, so they put it on the porch and played on it through the open window. Then he will sit back and work his way to the Caliph of Baghdad. . . . The firelight will get into your father's eyes and on his hair. He will move on from Baghdad to Big Bethel. . . . And you will hug your knees and hear the wind outside going its rounds among the snowy pines, and you will listen on till the story you are hearing becomes a part of the old winds of the world and the motion of the bright stars. And probably it will take two uncles at least to carry you to bed.

Sleighride Memories

Johanna Ter Wee

Moonlight bathed the sleeping land
With gentle, probing light,
And the breath from speeding horses
Formed great plumes of lacy white.
The runners made sweet music
As they moved in rhythmic beat
To the tune of crunchy, frost-spawned snow
Thrown far by homing feet.
And snuggled under blankets
So cozy warm, we'd share
A mystic night of beauty
And scenes beyond compare.
For the sparkling sheen of moonglow
Was a sight that seemed to be
A fairyland of shapes and hues
And endless mystery.
And even now on moonlit nights
I feel my memory turn
To youthful days, to sleighing days;
And once again I yearn
To capture long-lost pleasure
And hear as long ago
The hoof beats and the runners
As they sang in worlds of snow.

CHRISTMAS TRAFFIC JAM
Jane Wooster Scott, artist
Superstock

RAINBOW INN
HAPPY
HOLIDAYS
NOEL

Pears

On Christmas Morn

Adapted from an old Spanish carol

Ruth Sawyer

Shall I tell you who will come
to Bethlehem on Christmas Morn,
Who will kneel them gently down
before the Lord, new-born?

One small fish from the river
with scales of red, red gold.
One wild bee from the heather,
one gray lamb from the fold.
One ox from the high pasture,
one black bull from the herd,
One goatling from the far hills,
one white, white bird.

And many children, God give them grace—
bringing tall candles to light Mary's face.

Shall I tell you who will come
to Bethlehem on Christmas Morn,
Who will kneel them gently down
before the Lord, new-born?

SUSPENSE
Charles Burton Barber, artist, 1845–1894
Fine Art Photographic Library Ltd.

On Christmas Eve

Gail Brook Burket

We trim the fragrant balsam tree
Until the branches glow
With glints of shining ornaments
And wisps of sparkling snow.

We space the lights and silver strands
Of tinsel carefully
And climb to place the star which crowns
The tiptop of the tree.

We burn the yule log on the hearth
And gather round its cheer
To sing the carols long beloved
When Christmastide is here.

And at our window brightly shines
A gleaming candle's light,
Whose golden beams will shine afar
To welcome Him tonight.

POINSETTIA AT CHRISTMAS
H. Abernathy
H. Armstrong Roberts

The Christmas Light

John C. Bonser

I love the sight of Christmas lights
This season of the year,
The merry sounds that now abound
In melodies of cheer.

I love the words that can be heard
In carols that are sung,
The happy cries and sparkling eyes
Among the very young.

I love the scenes of evergreens
And wreaths hung everywhere,
Soft-falling snow and candle glow
And people bowed in prayer.

I love the bells whose glad notes swell
In tones of purest gold,
How goodness still our lives will fill
As God's great plan unfolds.

I love the light, that special night,
The shepherds saw afar
And ran to find, for humankind,
His bright and morning star!

A SLICE OF LIFE

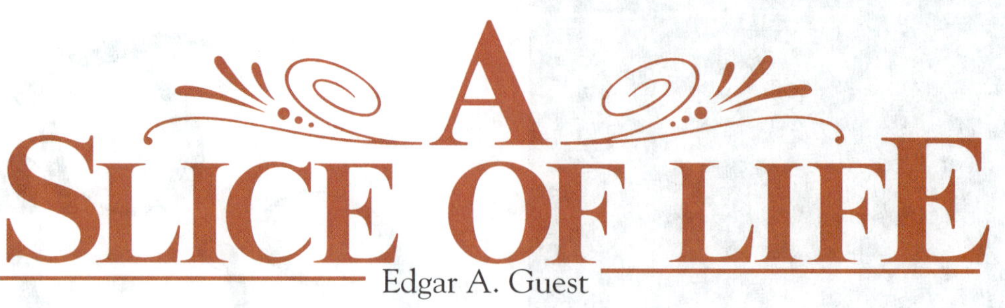

Edgar A. Guest

THE CHRISTMAS CAROL

God bless you all this Christmas Day
And drive the cares and griefs away.
Oh, may the shining Bethlehem star
Which led the wise men from afar
Upon your heads, good sirs, still glow
To light the path that ye should go.

As God once blessed the stable grim
And made it radiant for Him;
As it was fit to shield His Son,
May thy roof be a holy one;
May all who come this house to share
Rest sweetly in His gracious care.

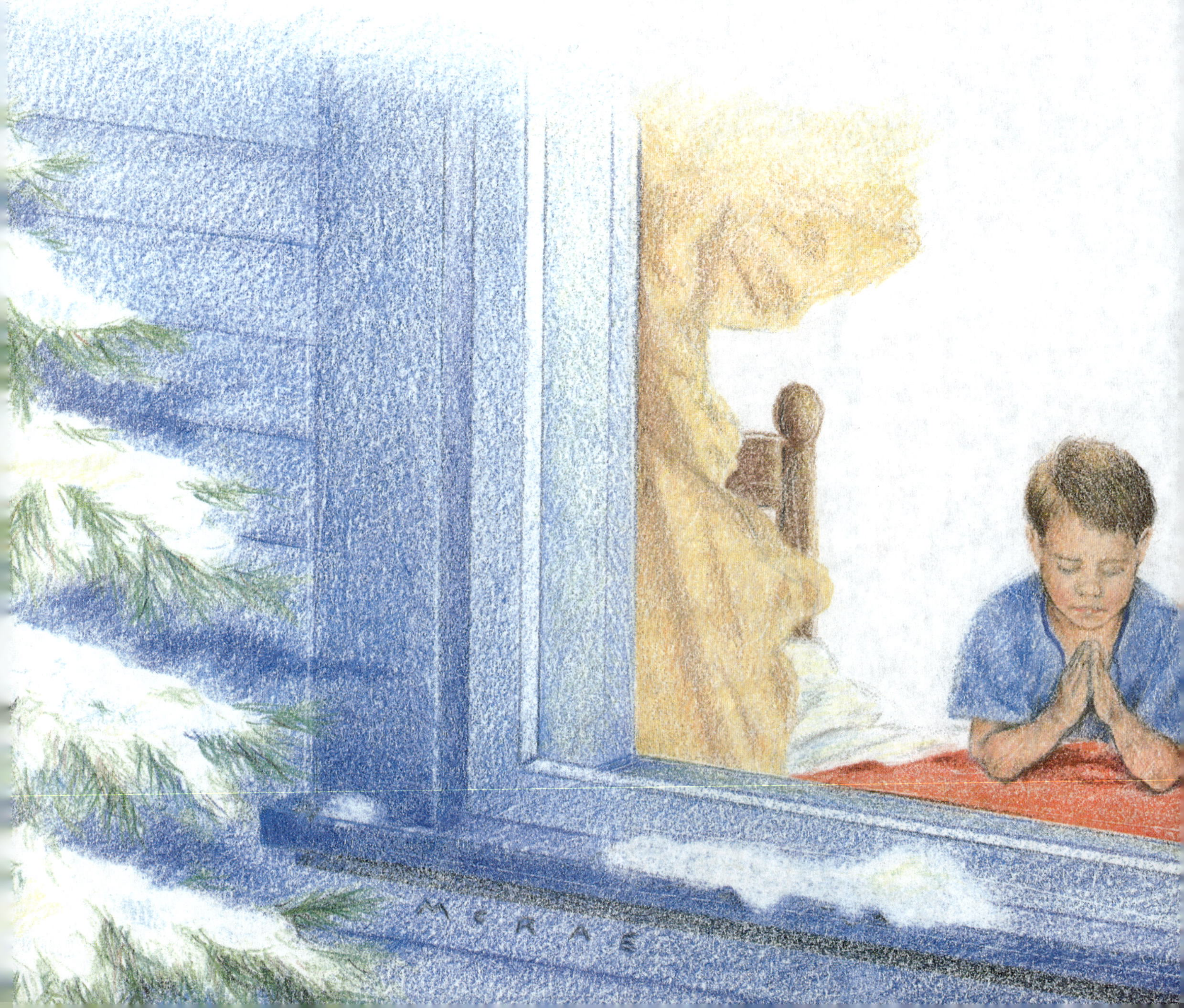

Within thy walls may peace abide,
The peace for which the Saviour died.
Though humble be the rafters here,
Above them may the stars shine clear,
And in this home thou lovest well
May excellence of spirit dwell.

God bless you all this Christmas Day;
May Bethlehem's star still light thy way
And guide thee to the perfect peace
When every fear and doubt shall cease.
And may thy home such glory know
As did the stable long ago.

Edgar A. Guest began his illustrious career in 1895 at the age of fourteen when his work first appeared in the Detroit Free Press. *His column was syndicated in over three hundred newspapers, and he became known as "The Poet of the People."*

Patrick McRae is an artist who lives in the Milwaukee, Wisconsin, area. He has created nostalgic artwork for Ideals *for more than a decade, and his favorite models are his wife and three children.*

The Stableboy's Story

Jean Conder Soule

"I have no room," the landlord said.
"No room for one guest more.
And you seek lodgings here for two?
Absurd!" He shut the door.

Sadly Joseph turned away
To face the gentle maid,
While tethered in the crowded yard
A weary donkey brayed.

"Come, Mary," Joseph spoke. "It seems
They have no room at all."
Then suddenly a boy appeared.
"Good sir, there is a stall.

"Indeed it is a rough-hewn place
Not fit for noble feet.
But the stable, sir, is clean and warm;
The hay is soft and sweet."

Mary nodded willingly.
"A stable will be fine.
I like the smell of fresh-cut straw;
I like the sheep and kine."

All his life a stableboy
Could happily relate
The story of a lonely pair
Who came within his gate,

And how, within a manger bed,
On hay as warm as fleece,
Nestled in his clean-swept barn,
There slept the Prince of Peace!

Pamela Kennedy

"And the angel said unto her, Fear not, Mary: for thou hast found favor with God."
Luke 1:30

"And the angel said unto them, Fear not: for behold I bring you good tidings of great joy which shall be to all people."
Luke 2:10

Fear Not!

A few Christmases ago, my mother sent us five beautiful new needlepoint Christmas stockings. Each featured a different holiday scene in lovely muted colors. They looked wonderful hanging over our stone fireplace, and I was delighted with them. My twelve-year-old daughter, however, was less than pleased.

"But our old ones were falling apart!" I reminded her.

"I know," she sighed, "but they were a tradition. I hate for anything about the holidays to change because I'm always afraid it won't be as special as before."

I could identify with her concern, because I also cling to the sameness of routines, relationships, and celebrations. There is a security in our traditions, and a value in continuing those that bring us meaning and delight. But too often I continue a custom long after its time has passed. Just as there is a time for every season under heaven, there is also a time for changing how we do things. In finding new ways to appreciate familiar situations and people, we discover things we might never have known otherwise.

When I look at the Christmas story in the Bible, I am reminded of how many people had to toss out their customary routines and expectations in order to participate in the adventure of faith God planned for them. Mary certainly had to change her views on things after the angel Gabriel announced she was to be the mother of God's only Son! And what about Joseph? From the account in Matthew, we learn he had to be reassured that it would be appropriate for him to marry his betrothed despite the fact that she was already pregnant. This was certainly in opposition to Jewish wedding traditions, which favored stoning or divorce for a woman who appeared to have broken her premarital vows. Nor was it customary to deliver a child in a stable, then cradle him in a cow's feeding trough! When the shepherds settled down for a quiet evening on the hills of Bethlehem, they hardly expected to be serenaded by a choir of angels and sent on a midnight trek to the city center. And even the Magi, after a grueling journey across the Middle-Eastern desert, were surprised to discover the King they sought, not in a palace, but in a tiny, nondescript house.

That first Christmas, nothing was in keeping with "the way we do things." But look at the results: Mary and Joseph learned to trust God in a new way and found His grace sufficient for all their needs. The shepherds witnessed the most marvelous event in history and became the first Christian missionaries. And those determined sages from the East found the fulfillment to all their dreams.

Could it be that we too would discover great and marvelous things if we were bold enough to cast off some of our tired, old traditions and dare to venture off into uncharted territory? How often do we limit God by insisting that He work in the same old ways? What if we truly faced the future with hearts and hands open to all the possibilities He might bring our way? It is true we could face some awkward situations. And we would probably be forced into uncomfortable circumstances. We might even encounter some unusual people—ones we might not otherwise meet. But then we would be in good company, wouldn't we? For Mary and Joseph, the shepherds, and the Magi all had to leave their comfort zones and step out into the unfamiliar too. I suspect God would tell us what He told them almost two hundred years ago: "Fear not!"

Lord, help me to be unafraid when You bring changes into my life. May I face them with grace and faith, knowing You are with me each step of the way. Amen.

HOME FOR CHRISTMAS
Superstock

SARAH
DEBBIE
NOEL

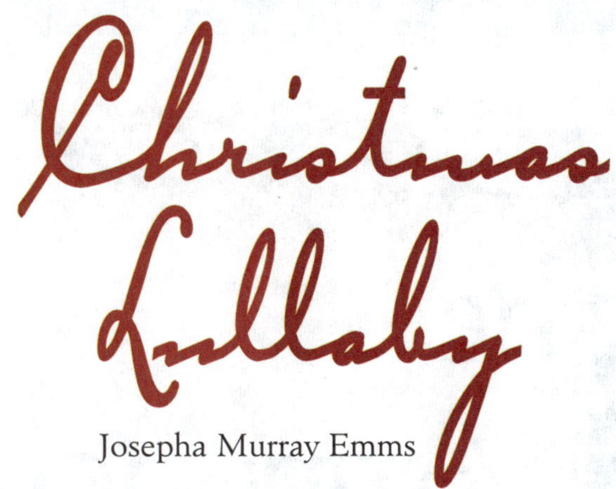

Josepha Murray Emms

O little One of Bethlehem,
You fill our hearts with cheer.
Each Christmas as Your birthday comes,
Joy sparks the atmosphere.

O little One of Bethlehem,
Above Your stable bed
Long years ago the angels sang
And blessed Your baby head.

While Mary held Your tiny hand
And Joseph knelt in prayer,
The shepherds stood in silent awe;
For love was everywhere.

O holy Baby! Child of God!
Dear precious ray of light!
Our hearts are lifted heavenward
This blessed Christmas night.

Birth Night

Mary Jo Dempsey

Soft, damp little curls and eyes drowsy blue,
A halo that's slipped just slightly askew,
Two tiny pink fists that move to and fro,
Small mouth yawning wide—a round, toothless O.

So straighten His garments, wipe off His chin,
And plump up the straw that He's lying in.
Let shepherds and wise men tiptoe to peep;
The King of the world has just gone to sleep.

MADONNA AND CHILD
St. Francis Xavier Cathedral
Green Bay, Wisconsin
Gene Plaisted, OSC/The Crosiers

The Annunciation

And in the sixth month the angel Gabriel was sent from God unto a city of Galilee, named Nazareth, To a virgin espoused to a man whose name was Joseph, of the house of David; and the virgin's name was Mary.

And the angel came in unto her, and said, Hail, thou that art highly favoured, the Lord is with thee: blessed art thou among women. And when she saw him, she was troubled at his saying, and cast in her mind what manner of salutation this should be.

And the angel said unto her, Fear not, Mary: for thou hast found favour with God. And, behold, thou shalt conceive in thy womb, and bring forth a son, and shalt call his name JESUS. He shall be great, and shall be called the Son of the Highest: and the Lord God shall give unto him the throne of his father David: And he shall reign over the house of Jacob for ever; and of his kingdom there shall be no end.

LUKE 1:26–33

THE ANNUNCIATION
Jacopo Tintoretto, 1518–1594
Scuola Grande di San Rocco, Venice, Italy
Canali PhotoBank, Milan/Superstock

The Visitation

And Mary arose in those days, and went into the hill country with haste, into a city of Juda; And entered into the house of Zacharias, and saluted Elisabeth.

And it came to pass, that, when Elisabeth heard the salutation of Mary, the babe leaped in her womb; and Elisabeth was filled with the Holy Ghost: And she spake out with a loud voice, and said, Blessed art thou among women, and blessed is the fruit of thy womb. For, lo, as soon as the voice of thy salutation sounded in mine ears, the babe leaped in my womb for joy.

And blessed is she that believed: for there shall be a performance of those things which were told her from the Lord. And Mary said, My soul doth magnify the Lord, And my spirit hath rejoiced in God my Saviour.

LUKE 1:39–42, 44–47

THE VISITATION
Jacopo Tintoretto, 1518–1594
Scuola Grande di San Rocco, Venice, Italy
Canali PhotoBank, Milan/Superstock

The Adoration

Now when Jesus was born in Bethlehem of Judaea in the days of Herod the king, behold, there came wise men from the east to Jerusalem, Saying, Where is he that is born King of the Jews? for we have seen his star in the east, and are come to worship him.

Then Herod, when he had privily called the wise men, inquired of them diligently what time the star appeared. And he sent them to Bethlehem, and said, Go and search diligently for the young child; and when ye have found him, bring me word again, that I may come and worship him also. When they had heard the king, they departed; and, lo, the star, which they saw in the east, went before them, till it came and stood over where the young child was. When they saw the star, they rejoiced with exceeding great joy. And when they were come into the house, they saw the young child with Mary his mother, and fell down, and worshipped him: and when they had opened their treasures, they presented unto him gifts; gold, and frankincense, and myrrh.

MATTHEW 2:1–2, 7–11

THE ADORATION OF THE MAGI
Jacopo Tintoretto, 1518–1594
Scuola Grande di San Rocco, Venice, Italy
Canali PhotoBank, Milan/Superstock

The Nativity

And there were in the same country shepherds abiding in the field, keeping watch over their flock by night. And, lo, the angel of the Lord came upon them, and the glory of the Lord shone round about them: and they were sore afraid.

And the angel said unto them, Fear not: for, behold, I bring you good tidings of great joy, which shall be to all people. For unto you is born this day in the city of David a Saviour, which is Christ the Lord. And this shall be a sign unto you; Ye shall find the babe wrapped in swaddling clothes, lying in a manger.

And suddenly there was with the angel a multitude of the heavenly host praising God, and saying, Glory to God in the highest, and on earth peace, good will toward men. And it came to pass, as the angels were gone away from them into heaven, the shepherds said one to another, Let us now go even unto Bethlehem, and see this thing which is come to pass, which the Lord hath made known unto us. And they came with haste, and found Mary, and Joseph, and the babe lying in a manger.

LUKE 2:8–16

NATIVITY WITH ADORATION OF THE SHEPHERDS
Jacopo Tintoretto, 1518–1594
Scuola Grande di San Rocco, Venice, Italy
Scala/Art Resource, New York

The Flight

And when they were departed, behold, the angel of the Lord appeareth to Joseph in a dream, saying, Arise, and take the young child and his mother, and flee into Egypt, and be thou there until I bring thee word: for Herod will seek the young child to destroy him.

When he arose, he took the young child and his mother by night, and departed into Egypt: And was there until the death of Herod: that it might be fulfilled which was spoken of the Lord by the prophet, saying, Out of Egypt have I called my son.

MATTHEW 2:13–15

FLIGHT INTO EGYPT
Jacopo Tintoretto, 1518–1594
Scuola Grande di San Rocco, Venice, Italy
Scala/Art Resource, New York

Christmas Eve

Anne Stubbe

Hushed was the night on the Judean hill.
The weary shepherds with their charges lay
Under a darkened sky, serene until
There shone the wonder of eternal day.
Then was the sky ablaze with glorious light;
The white-robed angels of the Lord came down:
"Peace on earth, good will to men this night . . .
Forever blessings on your little town."

Now, under centuries the shepherds lie,
And quiet is the little town, but still
The blessing holds. The word that will not die
Proclaims once more, as on that faded hill,
The love of God; and in the hearts of men,
The star still glows—and Christ is born again.

Shepherds' Song

Beverly J. Anderson

Infant Jesus in the manger,
Son of God and newborn King,
Filled with wonder we behold Thee;
Oh, that we had gifts to bring.

We are but poor, lowly shepherds
With no riches for a King;
As we kneel in adoration,
Loving hearts to Thee we bring.

Take our love and joy o'erflowing
And our praise of purest worth;
Simple shepherd hearts enfold Thee,
Little King of royal birth.

Promised One so long awaited,
How we marvel at Thy sight;
In Thee lies the world's salvation,
Gift of God born on this night.

SHEPHERDS BEHOLD THE STAR
Ted Hoffman, artist

THROUGH MY WINDOW

Pamela Kennedy

Art by George Hinke

Promises and Prayers

The morning sun turned the Bethlehem sky creamy in the chill dawn. Joseph woke and sat up, looking about the small cave in the dim light. Mary slept deeply, curled in the warm folds of her traveling cloak, exhausted from her travail and the midnight visit of the excited shepherds. Nestled in the clean straw, bound securely in swaddling cloths, the baby made quiet sucking sounds in his infant sleep. It was a placid scene, yet Joseph knew with the morning would come travelers anxious to tend their animals, beasts clamoring for food, and an innkeeper eager to have his stables empty of unexpected wanderers. Soon he must come up with a plan for his family. They couldn't remain in this cave for long, yet a trek back to Nazareth seemed neither wise nor appealing. Joseph stood and stretched, working the kinks out of his stiffened back. He would stroll about the inn, he thought, praying to God for direction.

Joseph measured his steps carefully, listening in the myriad morning sounds for the voice of the One who had guided him in the past. His thoughts tumbled about one another. He needed to register for the census, procure food and drink for himself and Mary, find someplace to live temporarily. His meager savings would soon be exhausted, and that meant he needed to find work as well. The words of David from the twenty-seventh Psalm echoed in his mind: "Wait on the Lord: be of good courage, and he shall strengthen thine heart: wait, I say, on the Lord."

"Yes," whispered the weary carpenter. "I will wait upon the Lord, for surely He will direct our ways." Renewed in hope, he headed for the inn to buy bread, cheese, and a little fresh fruit for their morning meal.

Mary, strengthened by the food Joseph brought, gently rocked her tiny son, humming a lullaby as He nursed quietly. "How long do you think we can stay here?" she asked her husband.

Joseph smiled as he gazed upon mother and Child. "I think it would be better to have human companionship," he replied, "although our current roommates have been most hospitable." Mary chuckled as a sheep bleated and a rooster greeted the sun with a well-timed crow. "I have some distant cousins here in Bethlehem, and perhaps we could stay with them for at least a while until the Lord directs us further," Joseph continued.

Mary nodded in agreement. "If it were possible, we could ask to stay at least until we take the Child to Jerusalem to be consecrated to the Lord."

Within a few days, Joseph located his relatives, who were happy to share their home with the little family. Mary, Joseph, and the Babe occupied a small room at the back of the house and enjoyed the warm fellowship around the family's hearth.

On the eighth day after the Baby's birth, Mary and Joseph bundled up their little Son and headed north on their six-mile trek to Jerusalem. Entering the city, Mary's eyes grew large and she held her Baby closer as the crowds near the temple jostled the little donkey on which she rode. Joseph tied the beast near the temple courts and purchased a pair of doves for the sacrifice. The family made their way through the worshippers coming and going on the temple steps. Sellers of birds and lambs hawked their wares, and moneychangers vied for customers. Here and there rabbis sat, teaching their attentive students. Mary's head spun with the noise and dust and smoke from the sacrificial fires. Which way should they go? It all seemed so confusing.

Then, as they entered the temple courts, a tall, elderly man approached them, holding out his arms to take the Child. It was as if the crowd stopped moving and the noises ceased. Mary looked into the eyes of Simeon, and a peace flooded her soul. Placing her precious Child in the old man's arms, she stood in silence as she watched the wrinkled face glow with joy.

Her heart stirred as Simeon's words echoed across the courtyard: "Lord, now lettest thou thy servant depart in peace, according to thy word: for mine eyes have seen thy salvation, which thou hast prepared before the face of all people; a light to lighten the Gentiles, and the glory of thy people Israel."

Mary glanced at Joseph as he stood beside her. His eyes were closed and his face turned up toward the sun. In her heart, she knew the confirmation of the annunciation she had received nine months before. Then she had been all alone in her childhood home; now she stood with her husband and Son, surrounded by hundreds of strangers. She wondered again at the sovereign God who would choose a young woman for so great a mission as raising His only begotten Son.

Simeon returned Jesus to her arms, then spoke with Joseph and her in reassuring tones. As he turned to go, the old man paused, and an expression of deep pain crossed his face. He took Mary's hand and spoke in words as soft as the breeze at sunset.

"And a sword shall pierce through thy own soul also. . . ." A chill of foreboding ran through her, and she looked at Joseph with questioning eyes.

Simeon slowly walked away, disappearing amid the temple crowds. The little family stood alone once more and turned to leave. At that moment, a tiny old woman, bent with age and walking with the aid of a gnarled staff, approached them. She introduced herself as Anna, a prophetess. Motioning them to follow her, she wove her way through the worshippers, leading Joseph, Mary, and the Baby to a quiet, shady corner of the courtyard. Here she spoke to them of many things, including the hope of Israel that resided in their arms. Tenderly, she stroked the Baby's cheek and gently kissed the sleeping eyes. Her own eyes filled with tears as she praised the Lord and blessed both Joseph and Mary before turning to go.

On the way back to Bethlehem, Joseph and Mary marveled at what they had witnessed and heard that day in the temple courts. In the months and years ahead, they knew their faith would be tested and their love severely tried; but in their hearts they would carry always the words of Simeon and Anna, words sent from God in assurance of His abiding purpose and plan. He who had begun a good work would surely complete it in accordance with His will. Joseph glanced over his shoulder at the dusty donkey he led. Did the simple beast know he carried the hope of the world on his back? The carpenter from Nazareth wondered at the mysterious and marvelous ways of God, then raised his eyes to heaven once again, giving thanks for answered prayer.

Pamela Kennedy is a freelance writer of short stories, articles, essays, and children's books. Wife of a naval officer and mother of three children, she has made her home on both U.S. coasts and currently resides in Honolulu, Hawaii.

Christmas Prayer

Alice Kennelly Roberts

There was a night,
There was a star,
There was an angel's song;
A busy inn
Too crowded then
For men to tarry long.

And on this night,
Beneath this star,
Across this wind-swept sky,
A sound went out
To still the earth—
A Baby's humble cry.

Grant us, O Lord,
The power to hear,
Above the worldly din,
The "still small voice"
Of centuries—
The voice of God within.

And give us, Lord,
The power to see
That light of lands afar,
The holy light
Of Bethlehem,
In every Christmas star.

It Isn't Far to Bethlehem

J. Harold Gwynne

It isn't far to Bethlehem
Where lies the newborn King;
It isn't far to Bethlehem
Where holy angels sing.

The wise men saw the guiding star
That led them where He lay;
The shepherds heard the heavenly song
That brought the better day.

We too may go to Bethlehem
And find the Saviour Child;
We too may hear the angels sing
Their hymns of mercy mild.

Our hearts are God's new Bethlehem,
Where Christ is born anew.
It isn't far to Bethlehem
If He is born in you.

SUNDAY SERVICE
Port Gamble, Washington
Steve Terrill Photography

Collector's Corner

Christmas Cards

by Lisa C. Ragan

I became a collector of Christmas cards by accident, really. Each December I feel a tickle in my stomach when the Christmas cards begin to arrive in my mailbox. I love to read the return addresses, the postmarks (some of places to which I've never been), and the beautiful designs of annual Christmas stamps. Some cards are sure to include annual letters from old college friends or snapshots of growing children. I inevitably feel familiar pangs of guilt when I see a card from someone I've forgotten to include on my own list, and I hastily jot down a quick note and send a return greeting. Through the years, I always saved a few special cards here and there from a faraway friend or beloved great aunt, until gradually I found myself saving more cards every year. Unbeknownst to me, my grandmother had also saved choice cards for many years and presented me with a shoebox full when she learned that I had accumulated my own collection. In her worn box I found antique cards from the 1920s and 1930s that featured cherubic children, a robin redbreast surrounded by ivy, and even a Father Christmas bearing holiday greetings. Some of the cards were still in their original envelopes, with postmarks from all around the country; one envelope featured a postmark from as far away as Kenya, where a distant cousin had once been a missionary. The assortment of old-fashioned designs delighted me so much that I began to seek out antique cards at nearby flea markets and from friends and relatives who had been around a few more years than I. Before I knew it, I had an impressive collection of Christmas cards.

ANTIQUE CHRISTMAS CARD

The oldest card in my collection looks more like a fancy Victorian Valentine than a true Christmas card. It was in the shoebox that my grandmother gave to me, and I believe it dates back to the 1890s. The front of the card features a drawing of a girl in a Victorian dress and hat. She is framed by a lace oval and additional filigree. Faded pink fringe along the card's edge adds to the Valentine effect. It is signed by someone named Margaret, but my grandmother no longer remembers exactly who Margaret was or why the card was kept these many years. I'm glad Grandma saved it, however, because it is now the star piece in my collection!

Since I've started collecting Christmas cards, I spend a little more time each year selecting the holiday cards that I want to send to my friends and family. And I make every effort to include a short note in each card. I can only hope that some future relative, generations removed from me, may stumble across one of my Christmas cards and choose to add it to her growing collection. I'd be honored to have my Christmas greetings so treasured!

FIRST KNOWN CHRISTMAS CARD, 1843. John C. Horsley, artist.
Commissioned by Sir Henry Cole, England.

ANTIQUE CHRISTMAS CARD.
Religious message. Unknown origin.

Collectible Greetings

If you would like to start a collection of Christmas cards, here are some interesting facts:

History

- The first known Christmas card was a lithograph designed in 1843 in London, England, by John C. Horsley.
- The success of the Christmas card in the United States is attributed to Louis Prang of Boston, who printed seasonal greeting cards in 1875 which were an immediate success.
- Early German mechanical cards often featured pull-down messages or even pop-up nativity scenes.
- Throughout the Victorian era, Christmas cards emphasized New Year wishes rather than Christmas wishes.
- By 1880, the popularity of Christmas cards had increased so significantly that prominent artists were commissioned to produce their own Christmas card designs.

Focusing Your Collection

Due to the wide variety of Christmas cards, many collectors narrow their searches to one category. For example:

- Focus your collection to a certain genre of Christmas cards, such as religious themes, comical verses, or even images of Santa Claus.
- Collect cards that typify crazes or fads of the time—model T's, hula-hoops, hair styles, popular songs.
- Group cards together that have unusual materials and/or features, such as musical cards, cards with pop-ups or fold-outs, or cloth or tasseled cards.
- Include a place in your collection for Christmas postcards, both old and new.
- Collect cards that support a particular charity, such as your local hospital or an international program like UNICEF.

Card Designers, present and past

Kate Greenaway
Norman Rockwell
Thomas Moran
Elihu Vedder
Jane Dealy

Card Makers, present and past

Prang
Rust Craft
Gibson Art Co.
A. M. Davis
Hallmark
Robinson Engraving Co.
International Art Co.

Christmas

Marlene E. Meehl

Red and green, the manger scene,
Snowflakes, snowdrift sparkling clean,
Holly, parties, eggnog toast,
Christmas carols, chestnut roast.

Tinsel, garland, trim the tree;
Open gifts, "Is this for me?"
Santa, Rudolph, fireplace flare,
Christmas stockings hanging there.

Children, Grandma, laughter, joy;
Cookies, candy, whirling toy.
Time to pause, to walk or ride;
Mittens, boots, new snow outside.

Midnight service, choir song,
Candle, hymn, devotion strong.
Silent thought, His spirit near;
Quiet worship, message clear.

Shepherd, hillside, watchful night,
Eastern star, His guiding light.
Camel, wise men, Bethlehem,
Gold and frankincense from them.

Joseph kneeling, prayerful nod,
Holy Baby sent by God.
Host of angels standing by;
Beams from heaven light the sky.

"Rejoice! Rejoice!" the angels sing,
"Hear the words of joy we bring."
Words of hope—true now, true then—
"Peace on Earth, good will to men."

MIDNIGHT SERVICE ON CHRISTMAS EVE
Peter V. Bianchi, artist

Ideals'

Family Recipes

Favorite Recipes from the Ideals Family of Readers

Editor's Note: Please send us your best-loved recipes! Mail a typed copy of the recipe along with your name, address, and phone number to Ideals magazine, ATTN: Recipes, P.O. Box 305300, Nashville, Tennessee 37230. *We will pay $10 for each recipe used. Recipes cannot be returned.*

Toffee Treasures

Spray 2 jelly-roll pans with vegetable-oil spray; set aside. In a heavy 3-quart saucepan, combine 1 pound (4 sticks) unsalted butter, each stick cut into 8 squares; ½ cup water, ¼ cup light corn syrup, and 2½ cups granulated sugar. Clip a candy thermometer to the side of the saucepan. Bring mixture to a boil over high heat, stirring with a wooden spoon. Continue stirring until mixture thickens, about 2 minutes. Using a pastry brush dipped in water, wash down sides of pan to remove sugar crystals. Reduce heat to low; stop stirring. Allow mixture to come to a boil. Boil, without stirring, until temperature reaches 280° F (soft-crack stage). This will take from 35 minutes to just over 1 hour; mixture must continue to boil. Remove from heat. Without scraping pot, pour mixture into prepared pans as evenly as possible. Using a spatula, quickly spread to a thickness of about ⅛ inch. Cool at room temperature 1 hour.

After toffee has cooled 45 minutes, chop 1 pound bittersweet chocolate into small pieces and melt in a double boiler over medium-low heat, stirring with a rubber spatula. Pour chocolate over toffee; spread with a spatula. Cool about 15 minutes. Finely chop 3 cups pecans; sieve to remove fine powder. Sprinkle nuts over toffee and press into the chocolate. Let stand at room temperature 24 hours. Carefully break toffee into pieces; or, using a large knife, lightly score into 2-inch rectangles and cut along scored lines. Makes about 70 pieces.

Ruth Pirtle
Madison, Tennessee

Wonderful Texas Candy

In a large saucepan over low heat, melt one 12-ounce package semisweet chocolate chips and one 12-ounce package butterscotch chips; remove from heat. Add 12 ounces cocktail peanuts and 3 ounces chow mein noodles; stir well. Drop mixture by teaspoonfuls onto waxed paper. Cool completely before serving. Makes about 4 dozen.

Betty J. Fox
Farmington Hills, Michigan

Quickie Fudge

In a medium saucepan over low heat, melt 4 squares unsweetened chocolate and 4 squares semisweet chocolate. Add one 14-ounce can sweetened condensed milk and ⅛ teaspoon salt; stir slowly until thickened, about 1 minute. Remove from heat. Add 1½ cups miniature marshmallows and 1 teaspoon vanilla extract; stir well. Add 1 cup chopped pecans; stir well. Drop mixture by teaspoonfuls onto waxed paper. Chill overnight. Makes about 1 pound.

Jean Fuller Kistler
Candler, North Carolina

Candy Cheese Gems

In a large mixing bowl, combine one 8-ounce package cream cheese, softened; one 3-ounce package lemon-flavored gelatin; and 1 teaspoon granulated sugar; mix well. Stir in one 7-ounce package flaked coconut. Chill until firm, about 30 minutes. Roll mixture into 1-inch balls. Roll each ball in 1 cup chopped pecans. Chill overnight on a tray lined with waxed paper. Makes 3 dozen.

Erin Broton
Dodge Center, Minnesota

Peanut Butter Fudge

In a large heavy saucepan, combine 2 cups granulated sugar and ⅔ cup milk. Stirring constantly, bring to a boil over medium heat. Continue cooking until candy thermometer reads 234° F (soft ball stage); remove from heat. Add 1 cup creamy peanut butter, 1 cup miniature marshmallows, and 1 teaspoon vanilla extract; mix well. Spread mixture into a buttered 8-inch square baking dish and let cool. Cut into 1-inch squares. Makes 64 pieces.

Francie Thompson
Delphi, Indiana

The Magic of Mistletoe

John C. Bonser

Do you recall the long ago
When underneath the mistletoe
We shyly kissed—young faces bright—
Within the log fire's blushing light,

And how, in after years, we knew
A wish of each that night came true
As riding homeward through the snow
Love blossomed from the mistletoe?

And still no season of the year
Seems quite as fair to me, my dear,
As that in which the crisp, cold air
Draws lovers closer everywhere.

And now that Yuletide's here once more,
I'll hang a sprig above our door.
For seasons pass, grandchildren grow;
There's magic still in mistletoe!

You Are My Christmas

LaVerne P. Larson

Dear one, you're my Christmas
Today and all year through.
You always make me happy
By what you say and do.
Within your eyes the Christmas lights
Twinkle all year long,
And in your merry laughter
I hear each Christmas song.
Your kindness reaches out
Like the loving evergreen,
And within your arms I find
A comfort that's serene.
Just as the star of Bethlehem,
Your constant, gentle love
Is like a Christmas blessing
God sent from heaven above.
My heart is filled with Christmas
As long as you are near;
The magic of your presence
Makes it Christmastime all year.

Michelle Prater Burke

Mormon Tabernacle Choir

Salt Lake City, Utah

Nothing gladdens my heart more than hearing a stirring vocal performance, especially at Christmastime. So it was with particular joy that I traveled to Salt Lake City, Utah, on a crisp December afternoon to hear the traditional Christmas concert of the Salt Lake Mormon Tabernacle Choir.

The choir evolved from the traditions of the Mormon pioneers who, in 1846, traveled west across the continent, singing hymns around the campfire during their journey. Soon after they arrived in the Salt Lake Valley in 1847, the Tabernacle Choir was formed; and in 1863, construction began on a permanent building in which the choir could sing. And what an amazing building it is. The tabernacle was completed in 1867, two years before the railroad reached northern Utah. Yet the settlers in this isolated community made use of Utah's natural resources to construct an awe-inspiring tabernacle that is now the home for one of the world's great musical organizations.

As I walk through the tabernacle's doors, I am struck by the impressive size of the place. Designed by a bridge builder, the massive roof rests like an enormous inverted bowl on forty-four columns of cut sandstone. The result is an auditorium which has a reputation for being acoustically perfect; a pin dropped at one end of the auditorium can be clearly heard at the other end, 170 feet away.

As stunning as the auditorium itself is the magnificent pipe organ. Recognized as one of the world's great instruments, the pipe organ was built of tall, straight-grained pine that was hauled three hundred miles to the site by ox-drawn wagons. Originally powered by hand-pumped bellows, the organ is now powered by electricity and contains eleven thousand pipes, including a few of the original wooden pipes.

As I eagerly await the beginning of this year's Christmas concert, I sit surrounded by thousands of other visitors to the tabernacle. Standing in front of the organ are the more than three hundred volunteer members of the Tabernacle Choir. Since their first performance in 1847, this renowned choral ensemble has delighted live and radio audiences worldwide. Suddenly, the organist begins and the combined voice of the choir rings out. The nearly century-and-a-half-old auditorium captures each note, and I am surrounded by the sonorous chords of my favorite Christmas hymns. And my heart sings along with every word.

THE SALT LAKE MORMON TABERNACLE CHOIR AND ORGAN
Salt Lake City, Utah
Photograph courtesy of
The Church of Jesus Christ of Latter-Day Saints

Christmas Comes Softly

Carol Bessent Hayman

Christmas comes softly to the waiting heart
In candle's glow and star and ringing bell.
Across the snow glad welcome lights the way
To hearth and home where joy and laughter dwell.

If what we are and what we hope to be
Could be one thing and that one thing be true,
It would be Christmas Eve—a waiting world—
And love's great miracle forever new.

The Quiet Things of Christmas

Carol Bessent Hayman

The quiet things of Christmas
Seep into our lives—
Cold December evenings,
Awesome starry skies;
The melody that haunts us,
The church bell sweet and clear,
The green and gold that forecast
The advent of the year;
The glad anticipation
As loved ones turn toward home,
Smiles on all the faces,
Hugs from those we've known.
The quiet things of Christmas
Set thankful hearts aglow
For light and warmth and fragrance,
Love and falling snow.

DUSK IN WINTER
Descutes National Forest, Oregon
Dennis Frates Photography

HANDMADE HEIRLOOM

HANDMADE ALBUM. Crafted by Mary Skarmeas. Jerry Koser Photography.

MEMORY ALBUM

Mary Skarmeas

With age, I find myself looking back more and more, remembering the people who have touched my life and reliving the joys, and the sorrows, too, that I have known. But often my reminiscing is mixed with regret—for there is so much about my childhood, about my parents, about life with my own children, that I don't remember or never knew. Of all the things I am thankful for in my life, the most cherished must be the close family ties that have anchored my life through the years; I wish today that I had had the foresight to ask more questions and to keep a journal of the passing of my own days. I was always so certain that I would remember what was important and always so busy raising my own family that I didn't have the time to sit back, reflect, and write.

So I decided that in celebration of Christmas this year I would create a special memory book. It would be my own personal stand against the passing years and the imperfections of human memory. On its pages I would record the thoughts, stories, and memories I want to preserve for my children and grandchildren. I first looked in bookstores at some beautifully decorated blank journals; but ultimately I decided that this special record required a truly unique book, and I decided to make it by hand. I had seen a bookmaking kit in a local craft store and was intrigued by the idea; my memory book seemed the perfect reason to look into making my own book.

In addition to the bookmaking kit, I picked up a few volumes on the history of books and printing from the library. I thought a little background would inspire me. I discovered that books in their modern form came into general use in the fourth century, when officials of the Roman Empire decided that pages bound at the side and enclosed by covers were more suitable than the traditional parchment or papyrus scrolls for legal documents and records. The new form of book was known as the *codex*, and its progress was furthered by Christian scholars who believed that since the documents of pagan culture were preserved on scrolls, Christianity would do well to adopt the new codex form for its writings.

Thus books took on their modern form and remained little changed for more than one thousand years. Each book was written or copied by hand, with illuminated letters and miniature illustrations added by skilled artisans. Much of the book copying was done by cloistered monks. It was a long, painstaking process that guaranteed that books were never plentiful and remained almost solely in the hands of the rich and the privileged. In the fifteenth century, however, a German named Johann Gutenberg revolutionized bookmaking when he invented the modern printing press. Gutenberg paved the way for the mass production of books and shattered the exclusive grip of the wealthy and powerful on information and knowledge. To this ancient history of bookmaking would I add one more volume, my own—a volume meant not to change the world or reach the masses but simply to enrich my own family.

I assembled my book from the materials in a kit; although the necessary supplies could be gathered independently, detailed instructions of one sort or another are necessary. If you'd rather not buy a kit, search craft stores and books at the library for good instructions. Most of the supplies are common enough items—good quality paper, sturdy cardboard, craft glue, fabric, staples—but you will need a book press, which can be either purchased or made. It consists of two lengths of wood held together with screws which can be tightened to press the pages of the book between the covers while the glue holding them together dries.

I began with the cardboard piece that would be my book's cover. Following the kit's instructions, I glued a piece of felt to the section that would be the front of the book and then covered the entire piece of cardboard with cotton fabric, folding the edges of the fabric over to the back of the cardboard. Then to create a finished look on the inside covers, I glued decorative paper endsheets onto the cardboard. I embellished the front of my book a bit with a second piece of cardboard, covered with fabric and edged with lace, which was cut slightly smaller than the front cover. I glued this second piece onto the front cover and, for a finishing touch, added an oval of fabric embroidered with the book's title. The book itself I assembled by stacking all the pages and stapling them together three times along the long edge. (It is wise to staple from both sides so as to assure penetration through each page.) The final step was to cover the stapled edge with glue and lay it along the center of the inside of the cardboard cover, where the spine will be. Once the pages were in place, I folded the book closed and placed the spine inside the book press to dry for twenty-four hours.

With the book assembled, I was ready to begin the real work of bookmaking—the work of my pen. Whether hand lettered on parchment or mass produced on a modern printing press, books from every age have a basic truth in common. They hold within their covers information that their author thought worthy of preserving. The pretty fabric cover and the clean ivory sheets of paper make my handmade book beautiful and unique; but the words that I have already begun to record on its pages are what will make my book a family heirloom—stories about my dear mother and father, favorite memories of my childhood, records of my own children's growth from year to year. Maybe the words I write won't change the world, and they certainly will not be read by more than a few eyes; but hopefully they will give comfort to someone who comes after me, someone who, like I do, enjoys looking back, and who, also like me, finds her memory in need of a little help.

Mary Skarmeas lives in Danvers, Massachusetts, and has recently earned her bachelor's degree in English at Suffolk University. Mother of four and grandmother of three, Mary loves all crafts, especially knitting.

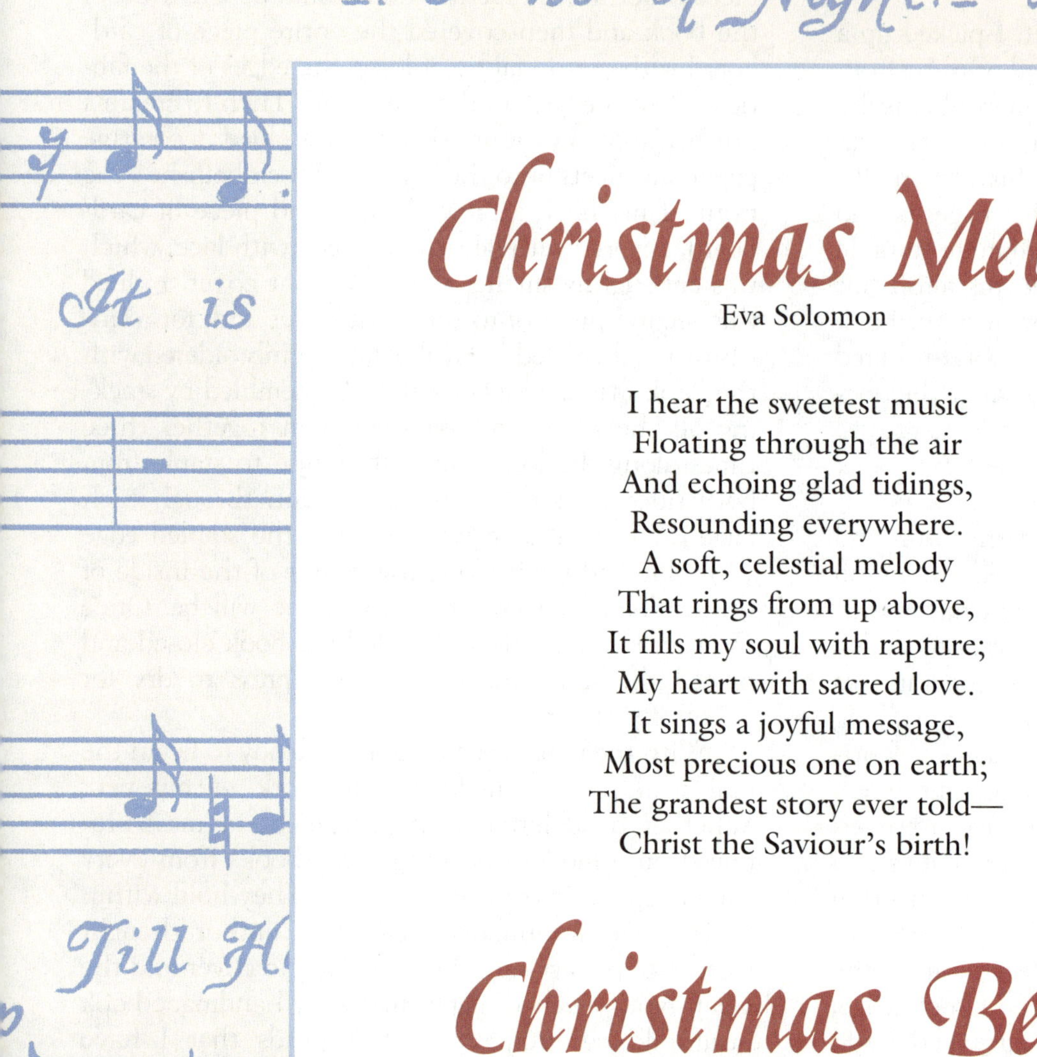

Christmas Melody

Eva Solomon

I hear the sweetest music
Floating through the air
And echoing glad tidings,
Resounding everywhere.
A soft, celestial melody
That rings from up above,
It fills my soul with rapture;
My heart with sacred love.
It sings a joyful message,
Most precious one on earth;
The grandest story ever told—
Christ the Saviour's birth!

Christmas Bells

M. Rosser Lunsford

Ring out ye bells of Bethlehem,
Ring loud this Christmas morn.
And toll ye of the King of kings
Who on this day was born.
Let every merry note be heard,
Ring praises of His birth,
Ring in the hearts of everyone
Good will and peace on earth.

A CAROLING TRIO
George Hinke, artist

Geo. Hinke

My Favorite Memory

Personal Stories of Treasured Memories from the Ideals Family of Readers

All I Want for Christmas

When December 1945 arrived, I had not seen my father for more than a year. He was a sailor in World War II, stationed in the South Pacific; and when the war ended, he was still required to continue his service.

As Christmas drew near, most people made preparations for an especially festive holiday with their loved ones home from the war. We had not received a letter from my father in a while, but my mother confidently awaited his return, assuring us he would probably be home a few weeks after Christmas.

Christmas Eve morning dawned gray with a winter storm approaching. By noon, heavy snow covered the county. We gathered around the Ashley heater after supper and listened to carols on the radio interspersed with weather bulletins as Mother would periodically peer out the window into the continuing fury. Soon after we settled into bed, I heard the sound of a car in front of our house. A door slammed and I jumped out of bed and ran to the porch.

Suddenly, a familiar voice called, "Gladys, honey, it's me!" Mother and I plunged outside and were engulfed in Daddy's strong, welcoming embrace. He had traveled across the United States on a grueling, train-hopping, eight-day trip to Virginia, where he telephoned his sister in North Carolina. She promised to have him home for Christmas if he rode the bus to her town. On their trip, heavy snow began to fall; but caught up in the homecoming surprise, they persevered onward. I shall always be grateful to Aunt "Santa" Ruby for helping make that Christmas unforgettable. For me, World War II ended the Christmas Eve night that my father came home to stay!

Louise Pugh Corder
Franklinville, North Carolina

A Special Christmas Tree

My favorite Christmas tree of all time was a six-foot orange tree that I had grown from a one-inch seedling. During the hot Arkansas summers, it sat in a pot out in the sun; and every autumn, my husband and I would take the tree to the school where I taught. The transportation of the tree became a family ritual, and my students loved watching it bloom and produce tiny oranges before their eyes.

One Christmas, our ritual was disturbed because asbestos was to be removed from the classroom ceilings during Christmas vacation. As I pondered what to do with my orange tree, I hit upon a solution. I'd take it home and use it as a Christmas tree! After some convincing, my husband helped me bring the tree home on a bitter cold Sunday afternoon. As we struggled to get the tree into the house, we wondered if we had lost our minds. Such a fuss over a plant! Looming in the corner, the weird, misshapen tree completely dominated the room.

We set to work decorating the tree with tiny red bows, white lights, and small red artificial apples. With the decorations and its own oranges, it made a striking Christmas tree! That year, the smell of Florida orange groves replaced the smell of pine in our home.

Bonnie Elders
Walnut Ridge, Arkansas

Silent Night

In the beautiful stone gothic church in the New England town where I grew up, we always ended the traditional Christmas Eve service with the singing of "Silent Night." One year, the girls' choir in the balcony sang a beautiful descant, written by Ethel Brandon, my daughters' choir mistress. The descant was as simple and as haunting as the lovely carol itself; and those fresh, young voices made it float over the top of the church as a sort of aerial benediction. At the end of the carol, men and women alike were wiping their cheeks.

Years later, one of my daughters related the story to me of how the descant came to be written. The minister, Fred Lorentzen, displeased with other available descants, began a campaign to get Mrs. Brandon to write one. She did write one, but kept it a secret until that Christmas Eve. On the third verse, her girls' choir gave forth with her descant. When the lights came on after the song, Mr. Lorentzen stood for the triumphant recessional with tears streaming down his face. Mrs. Brandon had touched his heart with her Christmas present to him and to the church.

The first year after Mrs. Brandon's retirement, my grown daughters and I returned to church for the Christmas Eve service, as did many other young women who had once been in Mrs. Brandon's choir. At the end of the service, when "Silent Night" was sung and there was no descant on the third verse, one of the young women began to sing the notes she had learned long ago from her beloved choir leader. All the rest of those who had participated in years gone by picked it up immediately. It stirred us all to hear "Silent Night" float over the church once again.

Julie Kuhns
Atlanta, Georgia

The Ugliest Christmas Tree

During one of my trips as a traveling salesman, I accepted an invitation to have dinner at a customer's home on a December evening in 1972. After dinner, their sons were putting the finishing touches on the family Christmas tree, a most peculiar specimen of greenery. The tree looked as if it suffered from malnutrition—its trunk was as crooked as a S curve on a country road and its top was broken. If it weren't for its greenish color, the tree bore no resemblance at all to a pine tree. My friend informed me that his family had decided to find the ugliest tree they could and give it a home for Christmas.

What a wonderful idea, I thought; it was the story of the ugly duckling, Cinderella, and Rudolph all rolled into one! They adopted a defected little tree and gave it love, dignity, and, best of all, the honor of being a Christmas tree. My family began our own "ugliest tree" tradition, which has now spanned more than two decades. Proudly we display our tree as a symbol of our love for all creation and a reminder that there was only One who was perfect, and His birth is the reason we celebrate this most blessed time of the year.

John Ray Greif
Saginaw, Michigan

Editor's Note: Do you have a holiday or seasonal memory that you'd like to share with the Ideals *family of readers? Send your typed memory to:*

MY FAVORITE MEMORY
C/O EDITORIAL DEPARTMENT
IDEALS MAGAZINE
535 METROPLEX DRIVE, SUITE 250
NASHVILLE, TENNESSEE 37211

There's a Song in the Air

Josiah G. Holland, 1819–1881 | Karl P. Harrington, 1861–1953

There's a song in the air! There's a star in the sky!

There's a mother's deep prayer And a ba - by's low cry!

And the star rains its fire while the beau - ti - ful sing,

For the man - ger of Beth-le-hem cra - dles a King! A - MEN.

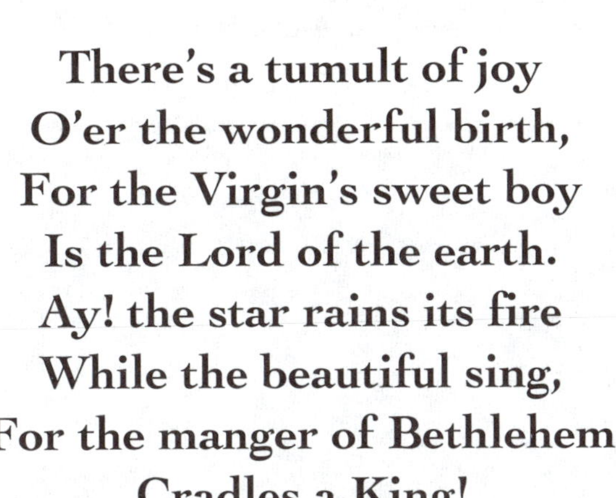

There's a tumult of joy
O'er the wonderful birth,
For the Virgin's sweet boy
Is the Lord of the earth.
Ay! the star rains its fire
While the beautiful sing,
For the manger of Bethlehem
Cradles a King!

In the light of that star
Lie the ages impearled;
And that song from afar
Has swept over the world.
Every hearth is a flame,
And the beautiful sing
In the homes of the nations
That Jesus is King!

We rejoice in the light
And we echo the song
That comes down through the night
From the heavenly throng.
Ay! we shout to the lovely
Evangel they bring,
And we greet in His cradle
Our Saviour and King!

NANCY J. SKARMEAS

JOSIAH GILBERT HOLLAND

Compelled by a simple philosophy and a knowledge of the ordinary problems of ordinary people, writer Josiah Gilbert Holland hoped to respond to the moral and spiritual needs of his generation. And it was through his hopeful and earnest works that he succeeded. In his lifetime, which spanned the middle sixty years of the nineteenth century, Holland became widely known and highly esteemed as a writer, editor, and lecturer; and he sold more than a half million volumes of poetry, essays, and other writings. In the second half of the nineteenth century, Americans counted Josiah Gilbert Holland among their most exceptional citizens.

Josiah Holland, the son of Anna and Harrison Holland, began his life in Belchertown, Massachusetts, in 1819. The family was poor, and Josiah's father, a hardworking yet thriftless man, held a series of jobs in a succession of western Massachusetts towns. Josiah Holland himself was slow to find his purpose. After high school he worked odd jobs for a time, tried his hand at taking daguerreotypes, taught writing, and finally entered medical school. Holland received his medical degree in 1844, but the profession never seemed to fit his character or to offer him any sense of fulfillment. His medical practice in Springfield, Massachusetts, foundered; and to earn enough to support his family—for he had married and had three children—Holland began to write. He was enthusiastic and even began publishing his own weekly paper, the Bay State Courier, but his early efforts met with little success. As the 1840s drew to an end, Holland finally settled upon a career that seemed to suit him and became a public school teacher and administrator, first in Virginia and then in Mississippi.

Holland liked teaching; it gave him the feeling of serving his community and provided an outlet for his newly discovered love of public speaking. But it did not satisfy his growing need for self-expression, which he had begun to indulge with his brief efforts at writing in Springfield. In 1850, Holland returned to Massachusetts to become co-editor of the Springfield Republican. While his partner in the editorial office took care of news and public affairs, Holland's job was to provide "human interest" material for the paper. Under the pseudonym Timothy Titcomb, he initiated a series of instructive articles on morality. These essays were later gathered into books whose titles—*Titcomb's Letters to Young People, Single and Married* and *Lessons in Life* were two popular collections—reveal the content and style of Holland's work. Holland's message was morality and spirituality as the source of answers to life's problems. His tone was instructive and familiar: "plain talks on familiar subjects" he called them.

The wide success of his newspaper essays gave Holland the confidence to throw himself entirely into a career as a writer, producing such stirring works as the patriotic poem "God, Give Us Men," whose words "A time like this demands/ strong minds, great hearts, true faith and ready hands" touched a nation. He wrote and published prolifically in the 1850s and 1860s; and his straightforward optimism found an eager audience in an America where life was changing rapidly and becoming increasingly complicated by technology, industry, and immigration.

Many Americans mistakenly believed that Holland was an ordained minister; but although his essays and later his lectures did often have the ring of a sermon, his message was not complicated by the details of any particular religious doctrine. Holland firmly believed that any individual could better himself and make a more valuable contribution to his community through attention to rules of morality. In 1869, after a lecture tour of Europe, Holland returned to the United States, settled in New York, and joined with publisher Charles Scribner to found *Scribner's Magazine*, which later adopted the title *Century Magazine*. Holland was now an editor and an author of wide repute, a man possessing wealth and fame, a man his contemporaries thought of as a voice for the ages.

Josiah Holland died from heart disease in 1881, leaving a lasting legacy both in publishing circles and in the hearts of his readers. The newspaper where he got his start in journalism, the *Republican*, remained a force in shaping public opinion in western Massachusetts for decades to come; and his magazine, *Century*, went on to become the most highly regarded literary periodical of its era. But as American life continued to change rapidly, new tastes began to read Holland's optimistic prose and poetry as simplistic; and his name eventually passed out of much of the public's memory.

But each year at Christmastime, many of us, though we may be unaware of it, sing the familiar lines from one of Holland's most treasured verses: "There's a song in the air! There's a star in the sky! There's a mother's deep prayer and a baby's low cry!" It was inspiring words such as these that touched thousands of American lives during the nineteenth century. Today, there is still much to be gleaned from the life and work of Josiah Gilbert Holland, and the philosophy at the core of his works is timeless. Holland's writings captured his simple belief that all people can make themselves better and thus make their world better; and even if the name Josiah Gilbert Holland is not as widely remembered during our century, his earnest convictions and the contributions he made to our country's literary history are memorable indeed.

Nancy Skarmeas is a book editor and mother of a toddler, Gordon, who is keeping her and her husband quite busy at their home in New Hampshire. Her Greek and Irish ancestry has fostered a lifelong interest in research and history.

little tree

e. e. cummings

little tree
little silent Christmas tree
you are so little
you are more like a flower

who found you in the green forest
and were you very sorry to come away?
see   i will comfort you
because you smell so sweetly

i will kiss your cool bark
and hug you safe and tight
just as your mother would,
only don't be afraid

look   the spangles
that sleep all the year in a dark box
dreaming of being taken out and allowed to shine,
the balls the chains red and gold the fluffy threads,

put up your little arms
and i'll give them all to you to hold
every finger shall have its ring
and there won't be a single place dark or unhappy

then when you're quite dressed
you'll stand in the window for everyone to see
and how they'll stare!
oh but you'll be very proud

and my little sister and i will take hands
and looking up at our beautiful tree
we'll dance and sing
"Noel Noel"

CHRISTMAS TREES
Near Monroe, Oregon
Dennis Frates/Oregon Scenics

Journal Entry: December 25

John Quincy Adams

[December 25] Christmas Day. No attendance at the office. I gave the day to relaxation, and, with a view to make an experiment upon the taste of the younger part of our present family, after breakfast I read aloud Pope's "Messiah," a poem suited to the day, and of which my own admiration was great at an earlier age than that of my son Charles, the youngest person now in my family. Not one of them, excepting George, appeared to take the slightest interest in it; nor is there one of them who has any relish for literature. Charles has a great fondness for books, and a meditative mind, but neither disposition nor aptitude for public speaking or correct reading. Charles must teach himself all that he learns. He will learn nothing from others. Literature has been the charm of my life, and, could I have carved out my own fortunes, to literature would my whole life have been devoted. I have been a lawyer for bread, and a statesman at the call of my country. . . . The summit of my ambition would have been by some great work of literature to have done honor to my age and country, and to have lived in the gratitude of future ages. This consummation of happiness has been denied me.

About the Author

John Quincy Adams was born on July 11, 1767, in Braintree (now Quincy), Massachusetts. As a young boy, Adams, the son of the second president, experienced firsthand the founding of the nation; he even watched the Battle at Bunker Hill from the hill above the family farm at age eight. Upon graduation from Harvard, Adams was appointed by President Washington as minister to Holland, and Adams went on to serve in the Senate; but it was during his tenure as secretary of state under James Monroe that Adams proved his skills as a statesman by drafting the legendary Monroe Doctrine. In 1825, Adams was chosen as the sixth president of the United States. After his single term, he was elected to the House of Representatives, where he remained a powerful leader for nine consecutive terms, earning the moniker "Old Man Eloquent" by speaking his conscience about moral issues, especially slavery. An avid scholar of literature and writing, Adams kept a journal for at least fifty years. He died at the Capitol building on February 23, 1848.

—Andrea Zywicki

JOHN QUINCY ADAMS
Superstock

Gliding as in Days Gone By

Helen Ehler

Today my yard is covered
With an ermine blanket, white;
The windowpanes are glistening
To each childish heart's delight.

Soon happy, frost-kissed children
Will a fort or snowman make;
They eagerly will welcome
Every tiny, crystal flake.

Out in the shed is waiting,
All painted rosy red
With runner slick and shiny,
That grand, new Christmas sled.

The anxious, bundled boys and girls
Soon down the hill will fly,
Unaware my heart is with them,
Gliding as in days gone by.

Snowmen

Carol Ann Kimball

A snowman stands
In our front yard,
A dirty, dripping sight,
With soggy scarf
And lanky arms
And mud all daubed on white.

Another snowman,
Quite the same,
But built a great deal stronger,
Stands shivering
On my kitchen floor
And begs to stay out longer.

SLEDDING DAYS
Richard Gaul
FPG International

The Doe

Carolyn E. Bailey

At once she knows I see her standing there
Where tidy lawn and tangled forest merge,
In winter's pensive hush, a vision rare,
As separate worlds of faith and fact converge.

When summer sings, our senses are replete,
The landscape of our lives so lush and green.
We do not hear the cushioned fall of feet;
The watchful silhouette remains unseen.

Her colors, soft, autumnal, subtle shades,
And movements motionless as stone or ice
Are armor to deflect men's vile crusades
And pitiless demand for sacrifice.

I open wide the shutter of my soul,
Engrave her image deep in memory
For days when harsh existence takes it toll
And love and hope and beauty turn and flee.

With gentle gaze she strikes my heart a blow
Of certainty as strong as tallest pine,
That though we seldom see, we still may know
The presence in our world of the divine.

Silence

Micki Warner

Gentle snowflakes,
falling
to a sleeping earth.
Dusting tree limbs
gently,
lightly clinging
whisper soft
upon the grasses,
building fragile towers,
and on the fur
of woodland creatures,
lasting but a second.

THE SISTERS OF CHARITY
Charles Burton Barber, artist, 1845–1894
Beaton-Brown Fine Paintings, London
Bridgeman Art Library, London/Superstock

Country CHRONICLE

Lansing Christman

New Year's Contemplations

Tap gently before you enter the door to the new year. I always do. I like to spend that last hour of the old year in the stillness of my house, listening quietly to the contented ticking of the mantel clock. At the midnight hour, I thrill to hear those twelve pealing bells marking an end and a beginning.

I have no need for a Times Square celebration with its clamor and din. Rather, I may play a record of Guy Lombardo and the Royal Canadians or Vivaldi's *Four Seasons* with its enchanting music. Or perhaps a book of poems will be my companion. I may choose Robert Frost or Whitman's *Leaves of Grass* or even my father's *Wild Pasture Pine*, which won the John Burroughs Memorial Association Award for best nature writing in 1934.

In the quiet of the evening during that final hour of the old year, I may choose to meditate and dream of a snow-capped hill sparkling in the glow of the winter moon. Or I may look out of the window to capture the glittering stars in the nighttime skies.

A night of wind will surely bring the rattling song of the shutters on my house or the creaking and groaning of trees in the bristling gusts. If the winter cold falls low enough, I am sure to hear the sharp cracking sound of frost tugging at the nails in the siding.

As I sit surrounded by my thoughts of the newborn year, I realize I have not faced a year in my life without some challenge or change. I have always found it best, therefore, to meet each year with optimism and trust, with faith and love in my heart. These four components comprise a deep spiritual part of my being. And with my faith in God, I find the sun shines even in the darkest of hours.

And so I wish you a happy new year full of sunshine!

The author of two published books, Lansing Christman has been contributing to Ideals *for more than twenty years. Mr. Christman has also been published in several American, foreign, and braille anthologies. He lives in rural South Carolina.*

COVERED BRIDGE
Franconia Notch State Park, New Hampshire
William Johnson/Johnson's Photography

Winter Labor of Love

Virginia Blanck Moore

There's someone waiting for me there
Amid the ice and snow.
So reluctantly I don my boots,
And out the door I go.
Into the biting wind I plunge
And over crusted drifts
Until I reach a sheltered spot,
And then my cold mouth lifts
Into a smile, for there they wait,
A hungry, feathered band,
For me to sweep the feeder clean
And answer their demand.
And answer their demand I do,
As they seem to know I will.
I pour the brown seeds liberally—
No matter if some spill.
Then warm of heart though cold of foot,
I enjoy my breakfast fare
With the knowledge that my feathered friends
Are eating well out there.

SUPPERTIME
Male Cardinal
Missouri
Gay Bumgarner

Readers' Forum

Snapshots from Our Ideals *Readers*

ABOVE: Cheryl DeKova of Vancouver, British Columbia, shares this picture of her own sleeping angel, daughter Katelyn, age three and a half.

RIGHT: Mrs. Ray Cline of Coeur d'Alene, Idaho, is the proud great-grandmother of this living nativity, which includes Loren, age six, as "Mary"; Michael, age four, as "Joseph"; and Taylor, age six months, as "Angel on High" (held securely from behind by her father). The children live with their parents, David and Jennifer Bjork, in Bismarck, North Dakota.

THANK YOU Cheryl DeKova, Mrs. Ray Cline, Judith Perry, and Lynn Brumm for sharing with *Ideals*. We hope to hear from other readers who would like to share snapshots with the *Ideals* family. Please include a self-addressed, stamped envelope if you would like the photos returned. Keep your original photographs for safekeeping and send duplicate photos along with your name, address, and telephone number to:

READERS' FORUM
IDEALS PUBLICATIONS INC.
P.O. BOX 305300
NASHVILLE, TENNESSEE
37230

ABOVE: Five-month-old Garrett Wayne Johnston, grandson of *Ideals* reader Judith Perry of Chesapeake, Virginia, enjoys playing Santa Claus for his first Christmas.

LEFT: Lynn Brumm of East Lansing, Michigan, wanted to share this picture with *Ideals*. Lynn loves to watch the antics of her animal friends outside her dinette window, where she saw this friendly squirrel satisfying his holiday sweet tooth with a candy cane.

ideals®

Publisher, Patricia A. Pingry
Editor, Lisa C. Ragan
Copy Editor, Michelle Prater Burke
Production Manager,
Tina Wells Davenport
Editorial Assistant, Tara E. Lynn
Editorial Intern, Andrea Zywicki
Contributing Editors,
Lansing Christman, Deana Deck, Pamela Kennedy, Patrick McRae, Mary Skarmeas, Nancy Skarmeas

ACKNOWLEDGMENTS

LITTLE TREE from *TULIPS AND COMPANY* by e. e. cummings, copyright © 1923, 1925, and renewed 1951, 1953 by e. e. cummings. Used by permission of Liveright Publishing Corporation. CHRISTMAS TREES from *THE POETRY OF ROBERT FROST* edited by Edward Connery Lathem. Copyright © 1923, 1930, 1934, 1939, 1969 by Henry Holt and Co.; copyright © 1944, 1951, 1958, 1962 by Robert Frost; copyright © 1967 by Lesley Frost Ballantine. Reprinted by permission of Henry Holt & Co., Inc. ON CHRISTMAS MORN from *THE LONG CHRISTMAS* by Ruth Sawyer, copyright © 1941 by Ruth Sawyer. Published by Viking Children's Books. Our sincere thanks to the following author whom we were unable to contact: Robert P. Tristram Coffin for CHRISTMAS IN MAINE.

May the true meaning of

Christmas

abide with you and yours this day.

Verse from "At This Time of Year" by Georgia B. Adams. Artwork: *LOVE SONG.* Original oil painting by Donald Zolan.